Original title:

Home Between the Walls

Copyright © 2025 Creative Arts Management OÜ
All rights reserved.

Author: Gideon Shaw
ISBN HARDBACK: 978-1-80587-056-2
ISBN PAPERBACK: 978-1-80587-526-0

The Echo of Warmth

Inside these rooms, a laughter rings,
Where socks go missing, and joy sings.
We dance in kitchens, no shoes allowed,
And somehow, we often attract a crowd.

In corners, dust bunnies have their say,
They witness our quirks in a fluffy ballet.
Coffee spills like wild confetti,
It's chaos, perhaps, but never petty.

Frames of Our Lives

We hang our pictures, a crooked line,
Each frame holds laughter and the odd whine.
The dog's in the family photo, what a sight!
He marches through life with woofs of delight.

Grandma's secret cookie jar, now a myth,
That vanished like socks, oh where is it?
We celebrate moments, both big and small,
In this gallery, we stumble, we fall.

The Scent of Togetherness

A whiff of baking bread warms the air,
As flour erupts like laughter, we share.
Spaghetti splatters, a culinary fight,
Tomato sauce on the wall? That's alright!

Our feast is a masterpiece, a bit bizarre,
With jokes served up like a side of char.
Each bite a memory, a savory cheer,
In this aromatic chaos, we hold dear.

A Safe Harborage

These walls may creak like an old chair,
Yet they cradle our dreams in their worn care.
We laugh at the cracks, the quirky designs,
Each little imperfection, laughter combines.

Under the roof, our stories unfold,
Of misadventures, both sweet and bold.
We stumble on slippers, we dodge the cat,
In this snug harbor, life's just like that.

Whispered Corners of Safety

In the nook where the cat naps,
The socks play hide and seek.
Dust bunnies have their laughs,
As I search, feeling so bleak.

My chair rules the space with flair,
It creaks when I tell a tale.
Imaginary thrones abound here,
As the remote goes on a trail.

I've found a treasure under cushions,
Old candy wrappers all around.
Each secret spot holds suspicions,
Of a snack that never made sound.

In the corners, dreams are spun,
Of wild adventures from the couch.
Every whisper laughs in fun,
As my plans brew like a slouch.

Hearths of Hidden Memories

The fireplace hums an old tune,
Where marshmallows once took flight.
Ghosts of snacks make me a buffoon,
Every ember sparks delight.

A warming glow, a melting smile,
As grandpa tells tales of his fame.
But you'll find all the cookies gone in a while,
Secret stashes, that's the game.

Potato chips in the drawers tight,
With notes that say, "Don't you dare!"
Each mischief hides in plain sight,
But who's counting? Not me, I swear.

Laughter lingers in cozy air,
With clinking cups and spilled tea.
Each memory, bold and rare,
Is a treasure kept just for me.

Shadows and Windows

The shadows dance along the floor,
As I tiptoe past with a grin.
The curtains wave, they want some more,
Of the drama that's brewing within.

The window sill is a stage for dreams,
Squirrels fight like actors in plays.
Through the glass, a world that beams,
With laughter echoing for days.

A shadow creeps in search of snacks,
Whiskers twitching, what a sight!
Behind every creak, a mystery cracks,
As I dive for the next bite.

In each corner, secrets sway,
Their whispers fill the room with jest.
Living in shadows, come what may,
Is just another funny quest.

Sanctuary of Solitude

The bathroom door is locked just right,
A palace for bubble-bath bliss.
With rubber ducks setting the fight,
I emerge, victorious in this kiss.

In pajamas, I reign supreme,
A fortress built of soft and snug.
The world outside is just a dream,
While I sip my tea and shrug.

The solitude hums a gentle tune,
As I dance with my thoughts in a whirl.
Wrapped in laughter beneath the moon,
Letting my imagination unfurl.

Each sigh is a giggle in disguise,
A haven where silliness plays.
In my sanctuary, joy never dies,
As I laugh my worries away.

Recollections in the Rafters

Up in the rafters, dust bunnies dance,
Tickling my nose, they start a trance.
Old boxes whisper tales of long ago,
Of socks that vanished, and the toys in tow.

There's a moth wearing my favorite hat,
As I search for treasures, I hear a spat.
The Christmas lights flicker, they groove with glee,
While the spiders argue, it's their party spree.

Haven of the Weary Mind

This is the place where all socks go awry,
Where lost remote controls seem to cry.
Cushions all gather for gossip and fun,
It's a comedy show, just under the sun.

The fridge hums a tune, a rap in its way,
While leftovers plot to have their last say.
Here's where laughter and mishaps collide,
In this little haven, there's nowhere to hide.

Threads of Us

In the fabric of moments, threads intertwine,
Stretched tight with Nutella, it's almost divine.
Grandma's old quilt, with patches so bright,
Tells tales of mishaps every cozy night.

The dog claims a corner, all fluff and snore,
While we pull two blankets, and battle for more.
Every frayed edge holds a secret, you see,
Of laughter and love, and occasional glee.

Shelter in the Everyday

The coffee pot's gurgle sings morning's song,
While the toast does a jig, it won't be long.
The cat struts his stuff, a king on a quest,
In this circus of chaos, we've learned to jest.

Dinner's a comedy, a recipe flop,
As peas roll away, they just won't stop.
We gather the ruckus, a mismatched parade,
In this shelter of laughter, adventures are made.

Lullabies of the Living Room

Socks now dance on the floor,
While the cat spies from the door.
Cushions throw a wild fit,
Echoes of snacks in every bit.

A couch that sings a tune,
Late-night giggles by the moon.
Remote battles on the rise,
Lost in laughter and surprise.

Tea spills like a morning breeze,
The clock chimes in with great ease.
Jokes tumble from lips so quick,
An afternoon sunshine flick.

Blankets hug in comfy ways,
As we snooze through lazy days.
Cushion forts rise, brave and tall,
In this laughter-filled sprawl.

Canvas of the Everyday

Paint splashed with the morning toast,
Brush strokes of a weekday boast.
Spills tell tales of breakfast fun,
While cereal races have begun.

Walls wear smiles and funny quotes,
Every picture, a story floats.
Scribbles on the fridge take flight,
In a dance of color and light.

Pajamas march in a parade,
As time for chores starts to fade.
Chasing dust bunnies down the hall,
With giggles echoing through all.

A canvas made of shared delight,
Each day's mishap feels just right.
In these strokes, we find our way,
Artful chaos in the play.

The Quiet of Closed Doors

What secrets lie behind that door,
Where whispered giggles gently soar?
Mad Libs filled with silly words,
Unfurling giggles like happy birds.

Snack packs hidden up on shelves,
Loud debates on who eats what else.
The couch holds tales we can't repeat,
More than a chair for tired feet.

Mysterious dust bunnies roam wide,
As laughter of friends starts to glide.
A treasure trove of quiet fun,
Until the door swings back, undone.

The world outside fades to a hush,
As our hearts fill in with a rush.
Moments stitched in softest lore,
In the quiet, we find much more.

Stories Stitched in Strips of Paint

Walls whisper tales of all who dwell,
Each brush stroke holds a giggle, a spell.
Colors clash like friends at play,
Painting memories in a wild array.

Bright hues clash with a gentle flair,
Each room's a laugh, a striped affair.
The hallway shimmies with cheer,
Echoes of laughter fill the atmosphere.

Splashes of joy on every edge,
A canvas where chaos makes a pledge.
We scribble stories, we weave them tight,
In this tapestry of pure delight.

So let the colors dance and sway,
As every strip shares a child's play.
In every corner, memories wait,
Stories stitched here are simply great.

Tides of Domestic Serenity

In the kitchen, chaos reigns,
A pot that bubbles, sauce that stains.
A recipe lost, a dinner gone,
We laugh till tears, oh what a con!

Dishes stack high, a leaning tower,
The sink's a swamp, what a power.
But in this mess, we find our cheer,
For every mishap, we hold it dear.

Echoes of Laughter in Gaps

Socks that vanish, where do they flee?
Under the couch, is it a sock spree?
We search in pairs, what a delight,
Our own sock circus, a comical sight.

Under the bed, the dust bunnies play,
The vacuum's fury, they scatter away.
Yet with each rumble, we cannot frown,
For laughter echoes, wearing a crown.

Havens Amidst the Chaos

The laundry sings a festive tune,
Colors clash, like a wild cartoon.
Oh what a dance, the fabric sways,
It's a fashion show of the oddest arrays.

Kids run wild, a tornado of fun,
With giggles and shrieks, on the run.
In this circus of love, we find our call,
Together we stumble, together we fall.

The Space Where Shadows Dance

Dust motes flutter, like tiny planes,
Chasing the light, ignoring the stains.
Shadows mingle, in playful delight,
Having a party, till the fall of night.

A cat on the shelf, with a critical glance,
Judging our moves, in a judgmental dance.
Laughter erupts, as we trip and slide,
In this wild chaos, we take it in stride.

Breath of the Unseen

In corners where dust bunnies frolic and play,
The missing socks audition for 'Hide and Stay'.
A chair's got a squeak, it tells all my secrets,
While shadows throw parties, they're experts in feats.

Waffles on Wednesday, they've found their new shrine,
A toaster that burns bread like it's training for mime.
Bouncing off walls, all the laughter takes flight,
With ghosts of my snacks keeping late into night.

Sanctuary of Solitude

In a nook full of pillows, I nest like a bug,
Wrapped in my blanket, it's snug as a hug.
The fridge hums a tune, it's a maniac's song,
As I launch my remote like it's a boomerang wrong.

A sneeze from the dust, and my cat darts like light,
Chasing her tail in the dim little night.
I giggle at shadows, they dance and they spin,
Whispers of mischief begin with a grin.

Footsteps in the Foyer

Mismatched shoes gather by the front door's dent,
They chat about journeys and where all they went.
An umbrella's sulking, it's seen better rain,
While scooters and tricycles argue for fame.

A coat rack is laughing, it hiccups in style,
Where hats make a mess, and it's all worth the while.
With each little footprint, stories unfold,
Of adventures and bloopers, both timid and bold.

Remnants of a Gathering

Crumbs scatter softly like whispers of cheese,
Where chips and dip tango upon the bright tease.
The sofa's now crowded, it winks with delight,
As friends share their tales over snacks in the night.

A sock puppet band plays on cushions' soft stage,
With laughter erupting, we're all in a rage.
Glow of the candles, the lights dimmed in cheer,
Echoes of joy linger long after they're here.

Light Through the Panes

Sunlight spills like spilled tea,
Pillows dance with glee.
A cat pretends it's a king,
While curtains flap and sing.

Dust bunnies hold a parade,
Old socks in the shade.
Squeaky floors tell tales so bold,
A saga of shoes, boots, and gold.

In the corners shadows creep,
Under the couch, secrets sleep.
A toaster pops with a grin,
As crumbs argue where they've been.

The fridge hums a funky tune,
With leftovers plotting a heist at noon.
Laughter echoes off the walls,
In this realm where chaos calls.

Echoes of the Unspoken

In the hallway, whispers collide,
Echoes of tones that cannot hide.
The dog snorts, dreaming in bliss,
While the fridge makes a suspicious hiss.

The laundry basket's a deep, dark sea,
Of unmatched socks, oh where can they be?
The broom waits, a silent knight,
Ready to wage dust wars every night.

Footsteps shuffle on squeaky floors,
Life behind the bolted doors.
A closet bears the weight of dreams,
In a universe of mismatched themes.

Dinner's a game, with pots that scream,
Where pasta's lost in a watery dream.
Yet in this curious, bustling space,
We find our joy, our silly grace.

The Fabric of Familiarity

Crumbs weave a story on the floor,
Like a quilt stitched with tales of yore.
A couch with springs that sing out loud,
Welcomes all in this cozy crowd.

Sweaters pile up, like a soft hill,
Each layer tells a tale at will.
Lost remotes hold a secret tryst,
In a battle of who gets missed.

An oven timer dings with flair,
While socks gather to form a pair.
The coffee maker hums a tune,
As mornings dance like a cartoon.

Pine cones from the yard, a crafty find,
Join the art show of a creative mind.
Here's where laughter and chaos blend,
In a fabric that won't ever end.

The Pulse of Private Spaces

Behind closed doors, giggles grow,
In secret corners, whispers flow.
A trampoline of thoughts takes flight,
While shadows bounce in soft moonlight.

Sticky notes detail every scheme,
Plans to plot the sweetest dream.
Beneath the bed, a monster lies,
Yet he's just after socks, not pies.

The clock ticks fast with a lazy beat,
Echoing tales of mismatched feet.
A light bulb flickers, trying to join,
The conversation of the playful coin.

Dish towels still hold debates,
Over who'll be the one who waits.
In these quirky, private nooks,
We write the funniest, heart-filled books.

Sanctuary in Shadows

In corners where dust bunnies dance,
Bright echoes of laughter find chance.
The fridge hums a tune, slightly off-key,
While socks stage a protest, just you wait and see.

Childhood drawings, crayon-streaked walls,
Exhibit a gallery where chaos enthralls.
The cat claims the chair as her royal throne,
And I sip my coffee, in my zone, alone.

The couch sinks lower, an old friend to meet,
In battle with crumbs from last night's sweet treat.
Spilled juice stains tell stories of joy,
As blankets conspire, a fort to employ.

With all of this mess, and laughter so free,
Who needs perfection? Not really, not me.
In shadows of comfort, we revel and play,
Our little sanctuary is brighter each day.

Embracing Enclosed Spaces

Walls whisper secrets of ages gone by,
While I'm stuck inside, with the TV and pie.
A dance with the vacuum leads to great fun,
As dust bunnies flee from my cleaning gun.

The hallway becomes a runway for flair,
My trusty dog barks, giving me flair.
With a twist and a turn, I pirouette wide,
In the confines of home, I'm a star with no pride.

Pictures hang crooked, a lovely delight,
They wobble and argue when I turn off the light.
In the glow of my kitchen, I concoct a feast,
Yet a burnt soufflé makes me laugh, at least.

Enclosed is amusing, a canvas of cheer,
We juggle our lives, draw laughter near.
With blankets and snacks, and the couch set just right,
In this snug little space, everything feels bright.

Fluidity of Life's Moments

In the living room, the laughter spills wide,
As plants on the window ledge swing with pride.
A dance-off erupts when the music plays loud,
And the cat joins in, feeling awfully proud.

Old slippers lost in the depths of the chair,
Keep secrets of journeys, the places we dare.
With a mug of warm coffee just spilling its cheer,
Each moment is fleeting but still feels so clear.

The kitchen's an arena, the mixer on blast,
As flour clouds rise like ghosts of the past.
We bake up sensations, yet all I can see,
Is a cake that looks more like a lopsided sea.

Laughter holds firm as we gather around,
In delicious chaos, our joy can be found.
The ebb and the flow of our everyday dance,
Life's little moments, we take with a chance.

Nurtured in Stillness

In corners of quiet, the cushions entwine,
Whispers of stillness where daydreams align.
A book with a promise, a mug in my hand,
The silence becomes art, a soft-hearted band.

The clock ticks softly, a heartbeat that sways,
While thoughts float on paper in whimsical ways.
Beneath the soft glow, shadows tease and play,
As I sip on my tea, the world drifts away.

Outfit choices peek from the closet's embrace,
Like fashion icons lost without grace.
A sock doesn't match, but does it even care?
The beauty of mismatched, a daring affair.

In stillness, I thrive, a proud little knight,
With cozy mismatches, I'm dressed just right.
With laughter that echoes through rooms near and far,
In these lullabies of life, I'm my own guiding star.

The Calm Amidst the Storm

In the chaos, socks collide,
Lost under the couch, they hide.
Cats march on, with stealth, they prance,
While kids throw toys, as if in a dance.

Dinner's a battle, peas take flight,
While laughter erupts, pure delight.
Spilled juice forms a rainbow trail,
In this circus, we laugh, we hail.

Laundry towers like a mountain tall,
Each week, it threatens to make us small.
Yet every mess tells its own tale,
Of love and chaos, we shall not fail.

So here's to storms, both wild and free,
Embracing chaos, that's the key.
Inside this whirlwind, we find our norm,
In the laughter, we weather the storm.

The Nest of Us

In a corner, the pillows grow,
Fluffy fortresses, a soft hello.
Blankets drape like clouds of cheer,
In our own nest, we have no fear.

We sip our cocoa, hats askew,
Tales spun from every silly moo.
The dog snorts loudly, joining the fun,
While the cat rolls over, basking in sun.

Crumbs scatter like pixie dust,
With chocolate fingers, we discuss.
Board games tumble, pieces in flux,
Life's a riddle, a lighthearted duct.

From giggles to grumbles, we find our way,
In this crazy nest, we forever stay.
Though the world outside may seem austere,
We're snuggled up with all we hold dear.

Cracks of Light and Love

Through shutters, beams sneak inside,
Dancing dust motes, a joyful ride.
Whispers echo, secrets unfurled,
In the heart of our whimsical world.

The plants lean in for a gossip spree,
While the fridge hums a symphony.
Silly hats graze on heads awry,
As giggles float up to the sky.

Cracks of light that gleam and show,
All the moments that make us grow.
Even the spills and laundry piles,
Turn into memories, laughter, and smiles.

Here's to the quirks that bring us near,
Finding joy, in every cheer.
With cracks of light that paint our days,
In this delightful, funny maze.

Sighs of Sweet Solitude

In corners dust bunnies roam,
Chasing my thoughts, they call me home.
A sock on the floor, a lone little shoe,
Life's little treasures, who knew?

Whiskers on windows, my loyal crew,
They judge my snacks, always in view.
The fridge hums a tune, a mad little song,
Calling me over, I can't stay long.

Spilled coffee stains my new white shirt,
I laugh it off, it's a comical hurt.
Beneath my humor, the chaos still reigns,
Yet laughter flows through my silly veins.

These moments so odd, yet perfectly right,
In this quirky space, I find pure delight.
Whimsical whispers from walls that confide,
In solitude's embrace, I giggle inside.

Timeless Echoes of Us

Echoes of laughter bounce off the walls,
Each silly memory, how time gently crawls.
A mismatched pair, we dance in a stew,
Spinning through chaos, just me and you.

Mismatched socks in our silly parade,
Each step we take, a memory made.
We argue with pillows, a culinary fight,
Whipping up madness in the soft light.

Chasing lost remote 'round the living room,
Trip on the rug, oh what a boom!
Giggles explode like popcorn on heat,
A carnival of joy in our quirky retreat.

Faint whispers linger, stories to tell,
In the dance of the odd, we do quite well.
With echoes of us in every room,
We paint our love with a splash of the absurd.

The Weight of Everything

The laundry piles high, a mountain of dread,
I search for my jeans, but I found my bed.
Each shirt a memory, each sock's a tale,
In this fashion fiasco, I might just bail.

Cooking disasters await in the kitchen,
A recipe's lost, my hopes are just glitchin'.
Coffee brewed wrongly, the taste goes awry,
But I laugh with my mug, oh me, oh my!

Juggling the chores like a mad little clown,
I stumble and fumble, but won't wear a frown.
The cat gives a meow, like she's seen it all,
In this circus of living, I stand proud and tall.

Though chaos surrounds, like a tornado's swirl,
In the weight of the mess lies a colorful pearl.
With a grin and a giggle, I face the day,
In this zany adventure, I'll find my way.

Serenity in the Silences

The quiet of morning drapes like a quilt,
A mug of warm coffee, the calm that I built.
Birds sing their sonnets; I laugh at the breeze,
In the stillness I find, it's just me and cheese.

A nudging pet begs for a snuggle to share,
As I watch the clock tick—does anyone care?
Moments of stillness, like pieces of art,
Crafting a canvas of humor and heart.

In odd little corners, laughter unfolds,
With daily absurdities—truth be told.
A sock puppet speech to the dust mite crowd,
In serene silly silence, I giggle out loud.

Oh how the echoes of quiet survive,
With comedy nested, I feel so alive.
In the hush of the hour, it's laughter I find,
In the sweetest of stillness, I'm happily blind.

Nestled within the Grain

In a nook where dust bunnies hide,
A sandwich was lost, and I cried.
The cat thinks the chair is her throne,
While I'm trapped in this zone all alone.

The fridge hums a tune, quite absurd,
The light flickers, yet no one has stirred.
Socks wander off to their secret lair,
Leaving me with mismatched despair.

When Aunt Mildred drops by for tea,
She brings stories that want to flee.
Her cats play tag with the doorknob's spin,
And I question how I let her in.

Yet laughter spills from every crack,
With witty remarks, there's no turning back.
In this quirky sanctuary I reside,
I wouldn't trade it, come what may, for pride.

Stasis of Loving Spaces

This couch is a treasure, oh so wide,
With crumbs from snacks we've tried to hide.
TV remote, a mystery vanishes,
The dog hoards treasures—what an odd wish!

Our fridge is a time capsule of sorts,
Backed by leftovers, and fungus of ports.
Every cork has a story to tell,
With wine spilled, I suspect it's done well.

The bathroom's a fortress where scents collide,
With toiletries shopping as our pride.
A rubber duck quacks out the plan,
As we navigate this space, hand in hand.

Yet through all the antics and strife,
These walls hold the laughter of life.
In this pause of hilarity, we find,
A joy that's sweetly intertwined.

The Fortress of Affection

Build a fort with pillows so high,
Toss in a blanket and watch time fly.
We giggle like kids at the sight of a speck,
Cockroaches fear us—what the heck?

The fridge is a treasure, a workshop of treats,
Where dinner's a battle and laughter repeats.
Sauce stains tell tales of culinary crime,
Yet somehow, we charm it into a rhyme.

Laundry piles up like a mountain of woes,
Each sock a memoir of mischievous shows.
When a shirt escapes, it winks and it pouts,
But in this chaos, our love truly sprouts.

We keep growing just like the dust,
In this wild romance, there's no need to rush.
So here we thrive, in our odd little sprawl,
A fortress of snickers, the best place of all.

Timid Footsteps in the Halls

Whispers echo as I tiptoe by,
Trying to wrap my head around why,
The cat's locked up where the food's displayed,
Meowing sweetly as purrs invade.

Down the hallway, the creaks start to sing,
A melody mixed with an odd little fling.
Ghosts of dust bunnies dance on the floor,
Trying to charm me to look for more.

The microwave hums a comedic tune,
Popcorn bursts echo, this isn't for noon!
What lurks in the corners, I dare not see,
But giggles arise when I finally flee.

All these odd happenings, silly and sweet,
In this quirky kingdom where nonsense meets.
With timid adventures through narrowest halls,
We find joy in laughter, come one, come all!

Murmurs of the Heartfelt

In a kitchen where chaos prevails,
The cat chases shadows, leaving trails.
Mom's cooking disasters, a sight to behold,
Her famous burnt toast, a treasure untold.

Laughter erupts as socks disappear,
The laundry's a maze that we all fear.
Caught in a dance with dust bunnies near,
Life here's a comedy, let's give a cheer!

Bickering siblings, we all play our parts,
Trading our toys and thoughtful retorts.
Each squabble dissolves into giggles galore,
The echoes of joy, we can't help but roar.

Yet through the chaos, love's always found,
In laughter and antics, we're joyfully bound.
These moments of madness, bittersweet and bright,
Make life a circus, a wonderful fright!

Within These Boundaries

Our living room's a battleground,
With pillows as shields, we stand our ground.
The dog thinks he's king, wagging his tail,
While we plot our next move, on a grander scale.

Grandma's chair creaks with whispers of past,
Reminding us gently, these moments won't last.
We jest about ghosts that roam in the night,
But they just laugh back, oh what a sight!

Chasing the rogue dust with feeble attempts,
We celebrate messes like grand monuments.
With crumbs on the carpet, a proud badge we wear,
In this carefree world, we haven't a care.

As we juggle life's chaos in jolly despair,
The love in our hearts is beyond all compare.
For within these limits, our spirits take flight,
We dance through the laughter, our souls full of light!

Whispers Beneath the Roof

The roof overhead holds secrets galore,
Like where Dad hid snacks behind the back door.
Squeezed in the attic, old boxes align,
Together we giggle, sipping on sunshine.

The clock tick-tocks tales from its cozy perch,
While Mom cools her heels, claiming she'll search.
But she's found a new show, entranced by the plot,
With popcorn as a pillow, she cares not a jot.

We feign innocence, cuddled on the floor,
As the dishes pile high, a familiar chore.
"Not mine!" we all chant, pointing with glee,
In this merry mayhem, we're all wild and free.

So here in this laughter, our stories connect,
Whispers and giggles, a tender effect.
With every mischief, our hearts intertwine,
In this sweet cocoon, all is perfectly fine!

Cradled in Confinement

Between these four walls, mischief does reign,
Where laughter echoes, like a joyful refrain.
A fort made of pillows, a space to explore,
Where we dive into dreams, adventures galore.

The fridge hums a tune, a bassline of sorts,
While the dog plots his attack on our shorts.
It's a comedy show, every day it's a blast,
With bubbling giggles and moments so fast.

Our 'artwork' decorates the walls with such pride,
Each scribble a treasure, we cheer and abide.
When bedtime approaches, we hide under sheets,
Trade stories of monsters, and laugh at our feats.

Though crammed in this space, it's cozy and bright,
Our hearts are wide open, filled with delight.
In the heart of this chaos, love finds its way,
Cradled in confinement, happy we stay!

Sheltered Stories

In a corner nook, where socks go to hide,
Lurk stories of dust bunnies, swaying with pride.
The fridge hums a tune, oh so sweet and loud,
A backup band for the snoring queen's crowd.

The couch has embraced too many snacks gone wrong,
With cushions that hold a strange, squishy song.
We dance in the kitchen, base of the cake,
Mixing flour with laughter, what a mistake!

The cat in the window, plotting her schemes,
While the dog runs in circles, lost in his dreams.
We giggle at pots, they clatter and moan,
In this playful chaos, we've found our own throne.

So here's to our sanctuary, filled to the brim,
With stories, and mishaps, and naps on a whim.
We cherish these moments, absurd but profound,
In our quirky castle, love knows no bounds.

Evenings in Reverie

When the sun dips low, and shadows come play,
We gather in the living room, come what may.
My tea's gone cold; it's a slick little prank,
As I spill it on details of our flair and rank.

The TV blares a soap, embracing the night,
While popcorn pops explosions, a glorious sight.
We argue about plots, who's right and who's wrong,
Yet laughter erupts like the stars in a throng.

The plants on the sill seem to dance with delight,
As they watch our debates in the soft-bulbed light.
Oh, the memories we weave, like old sweaters frayed,
Through the knitting of chaos, our bond is displayed.

As moonlight tiptoes in, with a smile just for us,
We share tales of nonsense, without any fuss.
The rhythm of evenings, that playful affair,
Wraps us in warmth, like a silly old chair.

Edges of Familiarity

The stairs moan loudly, like they're sharing a joke,
While the door sticks a bit—what a bothersome stroke!
We tiptoe and tumble in this cherished space,
Where every small mishap brings joy to our face.

On the wall hangs a clock, ticking time like a tease,
Counting moments of giggles, a breeze through the leaves.
With a dance on the rug, we train to be stars,
Making spectacles out of our Tupperware wars.

The fridge holds our treasures, leftovers of yore,
Remnants of feasts that have grounded our core.
A sauce splattered map of what we used to make,
Looks like a painting that nobody should fake.

In the corners reside all our odd, secret dreams,
Where whispers of laughter float soft through the beams.
Time nestles gently, a friend that won't fuss,
In these edges of comfort, it's always just us.

The Quiet Heartbeat of Us

In the twilight hour, pillows begin to conspire,
Whispers float softly, fueling our fire.
We share drowsy secrets wrapped up in delight,
While the cat claims our laps, as her throne for the night.

The floor creaks like laughter, a serenade slow,
As we trace the adventures of where we will go.
The walls catch the echoes of joy and surprise,
In this cozy oasis, we find our reprise.

Dishes pile high, a leaning tower of zest,
Challenges shrugged like a playful jest.
Beneath the stars peeking through windowpanes bright,
We revel in silence, the calm of the night.

With a heartbeat between us, both steady and clear,
We savor the moments, each chuckle sincere.
As the clock marks the hour, with joy we adjust,
In this space that we carve, it's all about trust.

Stillness in the Air

In a house that creaks and sighs,
The cat's the boss, we're the spies.
Dust bunnies dance, make no sound,
While the worn-out couch holds its ground.

The fridge hums tunes of past delight,
Leftovers plot a late-night bite.
Socks disappear, it's quite the game,
Hide and seek, oh what a shame!

The clock ticks loud, it's mocking me,
A minute's like an eternity.
Squishy chairs groan, they're quite the jest,
Come sit with me, we'll need the rest.

So here's to life, a laugh, a cheer,
In this quirky spot, we've got no fear.
With every quirky twist and twirl,
We find the joy in this odd swirl.

Nest of Memories

In a corner, where the dust and dreams,
Combine to make the silliest schemes.
Old photos grin, with mustached flair,
Telling tales of scandal, beyond compare.

The chair that squeaks, it tells no lies,
Of secret snacks and midnight pies.
Grandpa's stories flow like beans,
And grandma's laughter can tell what seems.

A rug that's worn, from many a fight,
It holds the secrets of day and night.
The quirky clock, it tilts to please,
Counting memories like falling leaves.

So here we sit, with tea in hand,
In this absurd and merry land.
Where laughter echoes, tears are rare,
We find our joy in what we share.

Rest Between the Edges

In the nooks where shadows play,
Ideas bounce and giggles sway.
The couch, like a cloud, is always near,
Whispering secrets that we hold dear.

The dog snorts loud with every nap,
Dreaming of chasing, a great big flap.
Remote control fights for our peace,
While popcorn battles never cease.

Outside the window, trees do sway,
With each soft gust, they dance and play.
In corners of plush, we laugh and sigh,
As the cat plots mischief, oh my, oh my!

So here we settle, snug and tight,
In the random chaos, we find delight.
With every tick and every tock,
This silly place is our magic rock.

A Canvas of Comfort

In a space where socks don't match,
And every corner has a scratch.
Paint splashed tales upon the walls,
And laughter bounces like bouncing balls.

The fridge has secrets, a tale to tell,
Of midnight snacks and pizza smell.
Each room a stage, we play our parts,
With quirky dance steps and happy hearts.

The laundry's a mountain, a summit climb,
In this colorful chaos, we pass the time.
Walls that cradle, and rooms that smile,
We'll stay awhile, let's stretch this while.

So raise a cup to this oddball scene,
Where silly moments reign supreme.
With every quirk, and laugh we hold,
This canvas of comfort is pure gold.

Comfort in the Corners

In the corner sits a chair,
Silently judging with its stare.
Dust bunnies gather, a furry crowd,
Chit-chatting softly, speaking loud.

Under the table, the socks have a dance,
Lost for months, now taking a chance.
They spin and twirl in the dim, warm light,
Join in their fun, it's a sock party night!

Crumbs from snacks, they plot and conspire,
Whispering secrets, their hearts full of fire.
The old lamp flickers, a witness to schemes,
As laughter erupts from the corners of dreams.

So we gather here, in the cluttered embrace,
Finding joy, in this chaotic space.
For in every nook, there's a story to tell,
A laugh in the corners, where all is quite well.

The Weight of Unspoken Words

There's a fridge full of stories, just waiting for me,
Eggs have opinions, just listen and see.
They quack and they chirp, but they're all just resigned,
To sit in the silence, no thoughts left behind.

The veggies get restless, in their crisp little rows,
Challenging each other with long-held woes.
"What's up with the squash? Why's the grape rolling 'round?"
Gossiping quietly, but no one makes sound.

Even the toaster has tales of its own,
Of burnt bread disasters and crumbs overgrown.
The kettle whistles, teasing the tea,
Wouldn't it be better if they'd all just agree?

Yet silence drapes softly like a big fluffy quilt,
With mysteries lingering about what was built.
But these unspoken words hang heavy in air,
As the fridge and the cupboard enjoy their old fare.

Sheltered in Stillness

The clock ticks slowly, mocking my time,
As I sit in my teacup, composing a rhyme.
Each minute's a puzzle, a riddle to crack,
Why do I hear the sandwiches laugh at my snack?

The shadows grow long, as I dodge the chores,
Hiding in stillness, avoiding the scores.
The dust motes waltz in the narrow sunbeam,
Finding my calm in a daydreamer's dream.

The chair creaks softly, holding secrets profound,
Of giggles and whispers that bounce all around.
In this quiet corner, the world feels so wise,
As I ponder the meaning behind all the sighs.

So I sip on my comfort, in the hush, I will stay,
For within each still moment, there's laughter at play.
With walls closing in, they wrap me so tight,
Sheltered in stillness, away from the fight.

Refuge from the Outside

Outside there's a chaos, wind howls like a beast,
But inside my fortress, I'm enjoying the feast.
The couch is my haven, it wraps me in fluff,
Ignoring the world, as I clench my snack tough.

The TV's a friend, with sitcoms that charm,
As popcorn's popped, I'm safe from all harm.
The curtains are drawn, creating a screen,
Against all the madness, they keep it serene.

The dog claims a spot, with an imperious air,
Guarding the territory, he's quite the affair.
Together we chuckle, at life's silly ways,
As outside there's a storm, but inside we play.

So let it rain loudly, let the thunder parade,
For here in this refuge, we've got it made.
With laughter and treats, we cozy and scheme,
Finding joy in the madness, and living the dream.

Between Timeworn Panels

In a place where dust bunnies thrive,
Old creaky floors try to keep the vibe.
The cat's on a mission, detective at play,
Chasing shadows that dance, in the light of the day.

Grandma would scoff at the strange sounds we hear,
Claiming it's mice, or a ghost that is near.
But really it's just the fridge's loud hum,
Making late-night snacks feel more like a drum.

Echoes of laughter, or whispers in jest,
Each wall holds secrets, and never takes rest.
The furnace is wheezing, the pipes sing their song,
In this quirky old den, where we all belong.

Let's dance with the quirks, giggle at the quirks,
For every odd sound, there's a treasure that lurks.
In the corners of chaos, where we invent our bliss,
It's not just a building, it's laughter we kiss.

Embrace of Forgotten Spaces

In the attic, there lives a troll,
Underneath boxes, collecting old soul.
A lamp has been searching for its shade,
Yet instead, it's creating its own charade.

The old couch holds stories, like loose change,
Once it was stylish, now quite deranged.
A fortress of pillows, a kingdom of fluff,
Making forts for our dreams, pretending is tough.

There's a clock that dances on the wall,
Ticking away as if it's having a ball.
The curtains are gossiping, fluttering free,
Sharing secrets of looming laundry with glee.

In every nook, there's a party, a spark,
Bouncing off walls, nothing seems stark.
With laughter like echoes that never fade,
It's a canvas of joy that we lovingly made.

Heartbeats in the Hallway

The hallway creaks like an old man's knees,
It whispers secrets, with every breeze.
A game of hide and seek with the door,
Making us laugh, it's a playful decor.

Dust motes flutter like fairies in flight,
Every corner's a stage for a comedy night.
The clock in the hall keeps telling the time,
But really it's just trying to keep up with rhyme.

We trip on shoes left about in the rush,
As the dog rolls over, making a hush.
While the walls tell tales of lost socks and shoes,
In this quirky journey, it's laughter we choose.

So here's to the hallways, a comedy show,
With each heartbeat echoing a sweet little glow.
In the spaces where chaos and laughter collide,
It's the heart of our lives, and we're full of pride.

Framework of Familiarity

In the kitchen, the blender starts to whine,
Like a stubborn old friend, through every dine.
The fridge hums a melody, sharp and sweet,
As we dance with the dishes, tapping our feet.

The walls are lined with photos and quirks,
Each face telling tales, with playful smirks.
A ghost from the past, with a wink and a grin,
Reminding us laughing is how we begin.

The ceiling fan spins like a wild disco,
As dust bunnies twirl, dancing low and slow.
We might trip on the rug, or spill our tea,
But in this framework, we're always carefree.

With every nook filled with bits of our lives,
It's a comedy show where everyone thrives.
Our laughter echoes, from floor to the ceiling,
In this place of familiarity, joy is revealing.

Memories Beneath the Roof

Once I lost my favorite sock,
It marched away, a little rock.
The cat just sat, with feline glee,
While I searched under every tree.

The fridge hums tunes of snacks to munch,
With every creak, it starts to crunch.
I swear the couch has secret charms,
It swallows me with all its arms.

The stairway whispers tales of haste,
Of trips and tumbles, never waste.
Each step a laugh from days long lost,
But I vow to reclaim my toast.

In corners, dust bunnies gather round,
With laughter echoing from the ground.
They plot and scheme for quiet fun,
While I can't find my missing gun.

Corners Where Hearts Reside

In the nook where shadows play,
Where laughter plans to slip away,
A pizza slice with extra cheese,
Hides dreams as light as autumn leaves.

The closet keeps my secrets tight,
Of costumes worn on Halloween night.
A wig that once danced, so divine,
Now terrifies with tangled twine.

Beneath the bed, a world so grand,
A sock puppet band begins to stand.
They play their tunes with squeaky cheer,
While I pretend I cannot hear.

A mirror grins with every glance,
Reflecting back that silly dance.
With every joke that life can glean,
I chuckle more, a giggling scene.

Embracing Familiar Shadows

The light switch plays its hide and seek,
Flipping moods from bright to bleak.
When it flickers, shadows talk,
Telling tales of a squeaky clock.

The kitchen sings with pots that clash,
While burnt toast adds a smoky dash.
A spoon that dances in the pot,
Sings of dinner, hot or not.

With every creak along the floor,
The house reveals a hidden lore.
An echo knows the words we use,
When singing softly, life's a ruse.

And in the hallway, dusty frames,
Capture moments, silly games.
From goofy grins to silly poses,
These snapshots hide, but laughter grows.

The Solace of Hidden Places

Old books stacked in a chaotic way,
Whisper stories that won't decay.
With cat ears perked for each soft page,
I read aloud, the cat's my sage.

In the laundry, socks twirl and spin,
An unending battle they rarely win.
They plot escape with every load,
But each time, it's me who's bestowed.

The bathroom mirror reflects my grin,
As toothpaste battles begin to thin.
With bubbles that giggle, splash and pop,
Who knew a scrub could make me hop?

In an attic full of distant dreams,
The old guitar still softly screams.
With every strum, a neighbor's yell,
They cheer my tunes, or toss a bell.

Whispers in the Corner

In the nook where the cat likes to snooze,
A sock puppet claims it can't find its shoes.
The plants gossip quietly, plotting a coup,
They're tired of being just little green goo.

The dust bunnies have started a union, it's true,
Demanding a raise for the things they accrue.
Last week they found crumbs from a loaf of bread,
A feast fit for rabbits, or—hey!—maybe Ted.

The clock ticks loudly, it mocks with its chime,
Every hour feels like a terrible crime.
I swear that the couch giggled once, maybe twice,
When I tried to sit down and rolled like a dice.

Under the stairs lives a ghost with a flair,
It dances with shadows that flutter like air.
It tells silly jokes from a time long ago,
But when asked for a treat, it just says, "No show!"

Shadows of Forgotten Spaces

In the attic there's a chest full of hats,
A pirate, a wizard, and ones for the cats.
They hold secret meetings—who wears what style,
While I take a nap and let them plot awhile.

The old sofa sits, feeling sad and alone,
It remembers the laughter and fun it has known.
Now it's a throne for the laundry to stack,
The dust bunnies keep whispering, "We want our snack!"

In the corners the creatures all gather and scheme,
A troupe of lost toys living out their big dream.
They put on a show for the mice and the shelf,
But with socks for a curtain, it's bad for their health.

The vacuum is silent, a monster by night,
It sweeps up the secrets—it gives quite a fright,
But if you look closely, behind it there's fun,
As it chases the dust bunnies—Oh, what a run!

Echoes of Silent Rooms

In the kitchen, the fridge hums a tune so sweet,
A symphony of leftovers—oh, what a treat!
Last week, someone tried to bake, oh what a mess,
Now the fruits on the counter are just under duress.

The chairs all complain when I sit down for meals,
They creak and they groan, expressing their feels.
I think they have secrets—we need a good chat,
They might be the wisest in this old spat.

Behind the door hangs a towel with sass,
It rolls its eyes every time I just pass.
"When are you cleaning?" it calls with a sigh,
But I just ignore it and give it a high.

In the hall, the shadows dance, tipping their hats,
They laugh at my tripping over my own mats.
With every misstep, they laugh and they twirl,
"Come join us," they shout, "let's give life a whirl!"

Haven Within the Frame

On the walls, there's a portrait—an old, silly grin,
It seems to chuckle each time I walk in.
It whispers of tales from the days long ago,
When people were silly and laughed with the flow.

In the bathroom, the soap gets jealous, I swear,
When the shampoo bottles get too much of air.
They fight for attention, it's truly a scene,
With bubbles and suds like a soap opera dream.

The floors, oh the floors, they creak like old grandmas,
Sharing their tales from 1980s jazz.
Every step is a rhythm, a funky old jam,
But trip on the rug? Oh, you're the family ham!

Under the table, a world full of dreams,
With forgotten crumbs and a few silver beams.
The chairs are enchanted; they spin and they glide,
As we all laugh together, our world is a ride!

Stories Woven in the Fabric

In the fabric of the day, threads collide,
A cat on the couch, the dog trying to hide.
Mismatched socks dance like they own the place,
While giggles echo, love leaves a trace.

The kitchen's a lab, experiments gone wild,
Spaghetti fears sauce, it's dreadfully mild.
A toddler's art graces the fridge with glee,
Danny's 'masterpiece'—stunning as can be!

Grandma's quilt holds tales from times oh-so-rare,
Each patch a chapter, laughter and care.
The closet's a jungle, where sneakers disappear,
Yet somehow that lost sock always is near.

In the attic, we find a tuxedoed rat,
He waltzed with a ghost, now just sits on the mat.
Amidst the mischief, sweet chaos unfolds,
Our tapestry's rich with forgotten, bright golds.

Memories Clinging to the Ceiling

The ceiling's adorned with sticky-note dreams,
Of elegant puns and glittering schemes.
A light fixture shimmies with each little shout,
Where laughter hangs thick, all worries cast out.

Once the dog jumped high, thinking he could fly,
Vacuum cleaner's chase—a fur-covered spy.
With each wacky tale, the walls just can't wait,
For wild memories shared, each odd little fate.

In corners, old toys gather dust and delight,
A robot named 'Chip' still wants to take flight.
But socks thrown in heaps by the little ones' game,
Are silent reminders that nothing's the same.

A shadow of charm dances with every glance,
As echoes of giggles and hiccups enhance.
Memories cling like stars in the night,
Each corner's a cosmos, our joy burned bright.

The Rustle of Quietude

In the quietude lurks a ticklish breeze,
If you listen real close, it snickers and teases.
Dust bunnies plot in their secretive waltz,
A mischievous mass, with some cotton ball faults.

The couch whispers jokes only cushions can tell,
With a puff of soft laughter, it knows all too well.
Mysterious crumbs from a snack long gone,
Host a party of ants till the break of dawn.

Windows creak softly, sharing tales of the storm,
As curtains shimmy lightly, keeping spirits warm.
The kettle's a chatterbox, full of hot dreams,
While teacups hold secrets in whimsical themes.

At night when the hush wraps the world in delight,
The walls start to chuckle, for all feels just right.
In the rustle of calm, life's laughter grows bright,
Hidden giggles abound through the soft, silken night.

Where the Heart Takes Root

Where laughter takes root, like weeds in the sun,
With jokes blooming wild, and tickles for fun.
The garden of mishaps sprawls in full bloom,
As wiggle worms dance with a hint of perfume.

In every adventure, a mishmash of smiles,
Grandpa's stories travel an infinite mile.
He swears that his goldfish could once ride a bike,
While Grandma just rolls her eyes with a pike.

The walls wear the colors of love's funny streak,
Where chaos breeds joy and mischief plays peek.
Beneath wooden beams, legends whisper with cheer,
While plants plot scenarios—our antics, they hear.

Here, where the moments entwine into fate,
Cereal mixes with laughter—oh, isn't life great?
The roots of our laughter reach deeper each day,
In a world spun from whimsy, we joyfully play.

Silhouettes Against the Ceiling

In the quiet of the night, they dance,
Shadows on the wall, a funny prance.
With every creak and every sigh,
The moonlit laughter floats on by.

A sock's adventure from floor to chair,
Two mismatched shoes make quite the pair.
Chasing dust bunnies, who knew they'd race?
Furry ninjas in this silly space.

The chandelier swings with a playful twist,
While spoons conspire in the silver mist.
A story told by a framed old cat,
While cushions chuckle, flat as a mat.

At the window, a sneeze from the tree,
Makes curtains giggle, oh so free.
Tonight's shenanigans, full of cheer,
In this goofy realm, we find our dear.

Secrets of the Supporting Beams

Once upon a beam, a secret's found,
A dusty joke lies underground.
The chandelier whispers tales in style,
Mixing laughter with a cheeky smile.

Oh, the ticklish cobwebs, how they tease,
Each corner hides a funny breeze.
A sandwich lost between the cracks,
Daring mice to launch their snacking attacks.

In the attic, a squirrel's bold heist,
Finding treasures that were once sliced.
While spiders share their gossip ways,
In the soft light of these silly days.

The beams chuckle with tales so old,
Of hiding places where secrets unfold.
With every creak and squeak, they share,
The laughter wrapped in our cozy lair.

Echoes of Sanctuary

Echoes bounce off the walls, quite absurd,
Whispers of laughter, softly heard.
A shoe with a secret, a coat with a grin,
In this playful space, we all fit in.

Lighthearted scuffles in the hallway dash,
With giggles erupting in a joyful splash.
A pillow fight breaking all etiquette,
Feathers drifting, oh, what fun to forget!

The fridge hums a sweet little tune,
While veggies plot in the light of the moon.
A dance of the pots, a waltz of the pans,
In our silly kingdom, we're all great fans.

And as the clock ticks, it joins in the jest,
Counting laughs, adding joy, it's the best.
In this echo chamber, life's little grace,
The heartbeat of our merry place.

Silent Corners of Belonging

In silent corners, mischief waits,
A quirky lamp, with funny traits.
Dust bunnies plotting their great escape,
While a bookshelf giggles in a literary shape.

A shoe's left behind, what a funky feat,
It's tried to leave but found defeat.
With a blanket fort rising tall and proud,
Where dreams and giggles are always loud.

Stale popcorn hugs the TV frame,
While cushions whisper a secret name.
The cat on the windowsill, plotting naps,
Laughs at the antics of endless mishaps.

Here in the corners, we find our cheer,
In every shadow, there's fun and a tear.
So let's celebrate this quirky spree,
In the soft embrace where we're wild and free.

Nestled Dreams in Nooks

In the corner, a cat snores loud,
Dreaming of fish, beneath a proud cloud.
A sock puppet talks with a spoon,
While the lazy dog hums a tune.

Dust bunnies dance with flair and style,
The fridge shares gossip, with a wink and a smile.
A moth on the wall tells tales so grand,
Of the crumbs he found, in a faraway land.

Lamps flicker, they have jokes to tell,
About the time they tripped on a spell.
A cactus giggles, roots tapping in glee,
While a spider hangs out, with a cup of green tea.

In this cozy nook, laughter spins bright,
Where socks find adventures in the night.
So nestle in, let worries unfurl,
In this whimsical, wonky, tucked-away world.

A Quilt of Small Moments

Pillows whisper secrets of dreams so weird,
Of sandwich summers, when all's been cheered.
Blankets chuckle at their crazed designs,
Spotting old stains and daring lines.

The kettle sings songs of forgotten lore,
About the time it boiled over the floor.
Teacups giggle with a sip and a clink,
While the tired couch starts to rethink.

A shoe is missing, dancing through the air,
While mismatched socks plot to have a fair.
Framed pictures wink in a silly embrace,
As chaos and joy take center space.

In these tender patches, laughter weaves,
Through simple moments and little reprieves.
So snuggle close, let the nonsense grow,
In this quilt of chuckles, where feelings overflow.

Timeless in Tranquility

A clock ticks slowly, with a smirk and a grin,
Counting down naps where mischief begins.
The turtle on the shelf rolls its eyes wide,
At all the chaos that it must abide.

Floating dust motes dream of the light,
Planning a rave once darkness takes flight.
Chairs swap gossip, creaking with might,
While the lamp leads the way, shining bright.

An old broom leans, with stories to tell,
Of sweeping up crumbs, oh how it fell!
Mismatched glasses toast with their chip,
As they laugh and they spill, on a playful trip.

In this gentle stillness, we find delight,
Where every shadow has a giggle in sight.
So breathe in the fun, let time wiggle free,
In this timeless place, just you and me.

The Breath of Walls

These walls, they chuckle in the dimmed glow,
Whispering secrets the floorboards know.
Meanwhile, the curtains have a gossip spree,
Trading tales of the neighbors' loud TV.

Light bulbs flicker, with a playful wink,
As they light the path where toys dare to shrink.
Pictures seem to giggle from their high perch,
As the rug hosts a dance, what a quirky search!

The doorbell sings, a high-pitched tune,
Inviting friendly faces, none too immune.
Tangled cords snicker, wrapped in their twist,
Throwing a party that none can resist.

In this quirky shelter, life hums a song,
Each corner a memory where we belong.
Let's celebrate this, with laughter and cheer,
In the breath of these walls, we gather near.

Refuge of Forgotten Laughter

In the corners, shadows dance,
Piles of socks in a silly trance.
Lost toys giggle, dust coats their back,
Stifled chuckles in a creaky crack.

The cat sprawls wide, a furry star,
Knocking the vase, what a bizarre!
Radiating joy, refusing to leave,
A kingdom of chaos, we can believe.

Teacups stacked in a haphazard tower,
Spilling stories with each passing hour.
Bubbly echoes from the fridge's hum,
Life's a circus; we're all just some.

Mismatched slippers strut in a race,
Chasing the echoes of an old embrace.
In this refuge, laughter's the key,
A carnival of memories, wild and free.

Cues of Comfort and Care

The couch is a ship, sailing through dreams,
While popcorn pirates plot daring schemes.
Under cushions, ancient coins gleam,
A treasure map drawn by a child's dream.

The fridge holds tales of midnight feasts,
A half-eaten cake, and crumb-laden beasts.
Sticky notes whisper sweet little lies,
While mismatched mugs are our same old spies.

The dog's on guard, holding down the floor,
Wait, is that a sock? Oh, it's just folklore!
Such comfort wrapped tight in a bumpy throw,
A gallery of antics, our feelings in tow.

With a thump and a crash, laughter erupts,
In this cozy chaos, love interrupts.
A place where quirks and warmth collide,
In this carnival of joys, we find our ride.

The Stillness of Unworn Paths

In the hallway, dust bunnies convene,
An expedition, silly and serene.
Scents of old pizza waft through the air,
Each step a memory, cluttered with care.

The shelves hold novels in ragged attire,
Pages whisper secrets of lost desire.
An old clock tickles, timing never precise,
Echoing laughter, advice without price.

Forgotten shoes lie beneath the bed,
A scuffle or two, stories left unsaid.
Each room a chapter, cluttered yet bold,
Mapping out antics of laughter untold.

The mirror reflects a face full of grins,
Light-hearted battles where silliness wins.
In this haven, quirk's the name of the game,
With each unworn path, we'll never feel shame.

Rippled Time in Aged Wood

The table creaks tales of a time gone by,
Where wild arguments and laughter would fly.
Chipped edges hold whispers of love and spill,
Come gather around, share stories until.

The bookshelf leans, a quirky design,
Hiding old tales of coffee and wine.
Every spine a friend; they all have their quirks,
In our joyous trove, nothing really lurks.

Chairs with wobbly legs keep us at ease,
Swaying with laughter like branches in the breeze.
Time is rippling, but it's all good fun,
In this wooden realm, we're never quite done.

The curtains flutter with a cheeky grin,
Revealing bright mornings where laughter begins.
In this orchestra of moments sincere,
We find silly rhythms that always endear.

Where Dreams Find Shelter

In the corners where socks go to hide,
A guffawing cat claims the place with pride.
The fridge hums a tune, a comedic delight,
As leftovers dance under the fridge's soft light.

A vase sings off-key, with flowers askew,
While the couch holds secrets, just me and my shoe.
A sandwich whispers jokes from yesterday's lunch,
As the blanket fort dreams of a grand avocado crunch.

The clock ticks away with a humorous beat,
While dust bunnies conspire to take over my seat.
The walls share a grin, whatever may come,
In this silly abode, I'm never alone.

So laugh with the shadows, and giggle with glee,
For here in this place, I can always be free.
With snickers and snorts, let the laughter unroll,
In this wacky haven, I find my true soul.

Lullabies of the Living Room

The couch serenades the day with a yawn,
As cushions plot mischief from dusk until dawn.
The TV flickers tales of wild, silly strife,
While popcorn kernels dream of a carnival life.

A puppy snores tunes, a melodic refrain,
As remote controls wage wars, driving me insane.
The rug plays hopscotch, a game for my feet,
While scatter pillows argue who's truly elite.

With laughter echoing through every dark nook,
Family snapshots play tricks, like a storybook.
The lamp softly chuckles, casting shadows on walls,
While I spin in my chair, in the laughter that calls.

So gather your giggles, share tales of delight,
In this crazy circus, we dance through the night.
For it's here in the chaos, where fun finds a way,
In this living room lullaby, we laugh at the fray.

Secrets Beneath the Eaves

Beneath the roof, where the odd socks dwell,
Whispers of mischief weave a comical spell.
The attic has jokes from the vintage parade,
As cobwebs and dust bunnies gloat in the shade.

Chairs chat about who had the wobbliest legs,
While old books giggle, sharing scandalous begs.
The air vents conspire to tickle my nose,
While shadows play tag, in dramatic repose.

Light fixtures tremble, they've seen far too much,
As plants plot to dance with a mischievous touch.
The windows are peeking, with eyes full of glee,
At the curious antics of critters in spree.

So let's listen closely, to whispers of cheer,
Filled with laughter and joy, that keeps us all near.
For the secrets up high, and the giggles below,
Are the funny little stories of life's grand show.

Fragments of an Inner World

In crannies and nooks, a world all its own,
Where chocolate crumbs gather, and wild tales are sown.
Jars of mischief stand guard on the shelf,
As I giggle and ponder my quest for more self.

The mirror reflects my attempts at ballet,
While dust motes dance like a comedic bouquet.
The daydreams wander, tripping over my feet,
In a universe filled with whimsical heat.

With every loud hiccup, the walls laugh aloud,
As socks form a chorus, a charming crowd.
Beyond those thin boundaries, life rambles and roams,
While I laugh with the echoes of silly tomes.

So let's twirl through the moments, so kooky and bright,
For this jumbled-up world brings pure, sweet delight.
In fragments of laughter, joy flickers and swirrs,
As I spin in this dance, of the nonsense that stirs.

Windows to Intimacy

In this cozy nook, where socks tend to hide,
Laughter echoes deep, like a joyful tide.
The fridge hums a tune, a song of its own,
As we dance with the dust, in our spirit zone.

A cat on the mantle, a dog on the rug,
Turns every little fight into a warm hug.
The coffee spills over, a morning delight,
In this chaotic dance, everything feels right.

Glasses on the table, filled with sweet dreams,
We gather our stories, like sunbeams in teams.
The walls, though they shudder, hold secrets quite dear,
In each playful quarrel, we find love sincere.

Beneath all the laughter, the world fades away,
With silly hand gestures that brighten our day.
In this world of quirks, where we freely engage,
Isn't life just a script, and we're on the stage?

The Fabric of Togetherness

Tangled in blankets, we pile up like stew,
Messy is best, and we all know it's true.
Lost spoons in the cushions, and crumbs in the chair,
These are the treasures that we all declare.

Pajama parties stretching till noon,
Popcorn fights that end with a spoon.
The blender's a band, making music with pride,
As we cook up a storm in this lovely ride.

The clock's ticking fast, it's already too late,
Time for some chaos, then time for a plate.
We giggle and chatter, share secrets galore,
In this fabric of life, there's always room for more.

As laughter stitches tight, the seams never fray,
We patch up our days in the silliest way.
With each tender moment, a patch to behold,
In this quilt of affection, our hearts stay consoled.

The Rhythm of Shelter

Inside our little square, the rhythm is sweet,
We shuffle and jiggle to the sounds of our feet.
The mop's our dance partner, the broom takes a lead,
While we spin in the chaos, our hearts never plead.

Burger night is sacred, with toppings piled high,
A race for the last fry, oh my, oh my!
We toast all our blunders with soda and cheer,
In the whirl of our antics, there's nothing to fear.

Each stumble a step, each burst into song,
We find our own tempo where we all belong.
From giggles to grumbles, the soundtrack plays on,
In this beat of togetherness, we've never been wrong.

So let's shake up the day with our foolish parade,
With cushions like confetti, and friendships we've made.
In the rhythm of love, we sway to our tune,
With the walls as our witnesses, we dance till the moon.

Embraced by Familiarity

In this quirky abode, where shoes lose their mates,
Stickers on the fridge share our dining plate fates.
An atlas of stains tells our colorful tale,
As we curve in our laughter, we don't ever fail.

Clothes on the line, like sailors set free,
Their flapping a language of soft camaraderie.
We joke and we jive, while bubbles invade,
In our sea of mishaps, we've happily strayed.

When chores turn to games in our sneaky crusade,
Dishes transform into towers we've made.
The broom's our great dragon, the mop, our sweet steed,
And with every small giggle, we tend to our need.

With moments so silly, they sparkle like gold,
In this humorous space, new stories unfold.
Though chaos surrounds us, we're gleefully bound,
In this knot of familiarity, joy can be found.

The Heart of the Threshold

At the door, a shoe pile grows,
Each one with a tale no one knows.
A cat in the corner gives me a stare,
As I trip on my laces, without a care.

The fridge is laughing, full of leftovers,
They whisper secrets like old-time lovers.
Dust bunnies dance like they own the place,
In this comedy, they're leading the chase.

Couches hold stories of naps long gone,
Where I plotted to conquer the lawn.
With every creak and groan of the floor,
The house chuckles, "You can't snore anymore!"

The doorbell rings, I jump with glee,
Is it fortune or just the delivery?
This space, a stage for my quirky play,
In every mishap, laughter finds a way.

Nestled in Familiar Nooks

Cushions piled like clouds in a dream,
Where I ponder and scheme with ice cream.
Books on shelves wink like old friends,
Whispering of journeys and how each one ends.

A mug that says, 'World's Okayest Cook,'
Houses my coffee and every odd look.
My kitchen's a symphony, pots softly clank,
As I create masterpieces too weird to rank.

Socks that vanish in the laundry's maw,
Are hiding, conspiring—is there a flaw?
With every search, I learn to embrace,
The little quirks that define this place.

Sunlight dances through the windowpane,
It tickles my nose like an old refrain.
Here in this nook, my laughter ignites,
Familiar and silly, my favorite sights.

Sanctuary of Lost Dreams

In the corner lies that bicycle,
Rusty and blue, yet still so full.
Dreams of speed and the wind in my hair,
Now it's a planter—how's that for flair?

Old trophies gather dust, they whisper,
"Did you forget us, or did you just fester?"
Each accolade has a tale to spin,
Of kid-like glory and where we've been.

The attic sings of hats from the past,
Each one a character, none unsurpassed.
As I try them on, I burst out in glee,
A mad hatter's tea party, just for me!

In this strange sanctuary, I claim my space,
With laughter that echoes and leaves a trace.
For every lost dream, a whimsical spark,
In the theater of life, I'm the leading arc.

Walls that Hold Our Secrets

Oh, these walls have ears, they giggle and sway,
Keeping my blunders tucked safely away.
They've heard my rants and my joyful chats,
And yes, the day I adopted six cats!

In the bathroom, the shower sings loud,
A concert of nonsense, I'm so very proud.
Echoes and laughter, my audience small,
But they cheer for me, as I trip on the wall.

Each scratch and dent tells a silent story,
Of baking fails and moments of glory.
The paint may peel, but the memories stick,
In this quirky circus, life's a comedy flick.

So here's to the walls, the keepers of fun,
And to all the secrets they hide, one by one.
May laughter ring out in rooms big and small,
For the best punchlines are shared with them all.

www.ingramcontent.com/pod-product-compliance
Lightning Source LLC
Chambersburg PA
CBHW050305120526
44590CB00016B/2495